AF224068

B&B
PUBLISHING CO

Library of Congress Catalog Card Number
This book has been published by B&B Publishing Co. Contact us for publishing needs.
469-632-6384

WAKEUP

I can do all things through CHRIST JESUS who strengthens me

God did not give me a spirit of fear But of Power Love and a Sound mind

I am Fearfully and wonderfully made

no weapon formed against me shall prosper

ELISHA CARSON

WAKEUP

ELISHA CARSON

Contents

My Mission

My mission is to encourage others to find peace and strength in any situation while also promoting purpose, growth, self-worth, and fruitfulness. I was once fighting a losing battle to be at peace to enjoy my life on life's terms and to satisfy my need for fulfillment and purpose. I can remember as a teenager taking solace in things, I once took for granted after becoming an adult such as writing poetry, making time to be creative, setting and reaching goals, building, and cherishing relationships. I was depressed, emotionally, and mentally defeated, I didn't see or understand my purpose outside of survival. I was not assured I could write again, get a better job, survive outside of the relationship I was in, or change my current situation. I cried out to God desperate for peace and change. It seemed like I was in an uphill losing battle and every time I had free time, away from work, or to myself, it was spent wallowing in pain and disappointment feeling sorry for myself. Instead of managing my time using my gifts, developing relationships with my children, and most importantly with God, I would be drinking excessively or doing something mood-altering trying to escape my reality. Spending more time seeking God and begging him for change in my life focusing on anything Godly whether it was music, a prophetic Facebook live, or a daily devotional, as I sought God, he gave me a revelation. This is information that is readily available to us all. God gave me the strength to fight through the pain, I was experiencing, through his word and by faith. God gave me an understanding of how forgiveness, spending time on his word, and taking actions would benefit his kingdom and my life. I was able to forgive myself and others and to let go of pain from an absent father, an unfaithful partner, and betrayal from people, whom I thought were my friends. I want you to be inspired and to be empowered. Not only am I free from alcohol addiction, but also free from depression. I can enjoy my life knowing that God is the true living water. I can work towards fulfilling my purpose big or small knowing that God is in control and that he can bless me with the desires of my heart as I seek to please him and to do his will.

I hope that reading this book will draw you closer to God and that he will give you a spiritual awakening, an aha moment, that will bring you peace and growth. I want my readers to tap back into their God-given talents and gifts and start seeing their God-given purpose as a way to benefit humanity, to please God, and to promote self-worth.

As I was going through my Twitter account looking back at my tweets, I realized how much time had passed! Logging on to Twitter, after years had gone by, I came across a tweet that I posted about a book I was planning to write, but I couldn't write. I also noticed a tweet from a childhood RnB singer and songwriter Sammie; he was working on a song called Insomnia around the same time. Years ago, he was singing as a kid and now as a young adult, he was still diligently working on music. It was then, the reality hit me! Something in my spirit was awakened. I realized years had passed and the dreams that were once goals were now just old abandoned thoughts. Like a treasure hidden and lost at sea, I lost sight of the dream to write. Unable to make and find time to nourish the seed that I planted, my dream died like a neglected fruit tree. I dedicate this book to God for putting it on my heart, to my children and family for being my motivation, to Deborah Hill for encouraging me and Sammie Leigh Bush for inspiring me with his perseverance.

Today working and living to survive has become the new norm, poverty is all too common. The purpose has somehow been replaced with disparity and survival. While our mental, spiritual, and physical battles include depression, addiction, eating disorders, and sexual obsession, we often overlook silent killers like stress, fear, rejection, and insecurities that can also lead to mental illness or far worst, suicide.

Nearly, 350 million people around the world are suffering from depression alone, according to *Bridges to Recovery*. We as in humanity have been robbed of so many intangible assets including time, love, peace, health, spiritual fitness, self-discipline, and hope. Too many of us are living just to get by when there is so much more peace and purpose a few feet away, all we need to do is reach. Taking a few minutes to act can make all the difference whether to experience the gift of life Christ offers us or the bitter struggle of survival without purpose and peace.

While it is important to survive, to work, it is most important to seek God. How can we possibly know we are doing what we are called to do or living our best life unless we seek God? Who knows better than our creator. Settling for the bare minimum without peace, growth, and joy may be good enough for some people but I believe many of us want and deserve a better quality of life mentally, physically, and spiritually but are too stuck in survival mode to get it.

While work life seems to be the simplest of topics when it comes to settling, we sometimes choose to settle for less in other ways. For example, we may choose to settle for a bad habit instead of working towards self-discipline. Staying in a bad or unhealthy relationship can be settling. Trying to fill a God-sized hole with a man-made solution is one of the most common ways we settle. Regardless, if you have a dream or passion that God placed in you or if you simply want to find self-worth and live out your destiny, and stop settling for less, then it is time to wake up and start living.

In what areas of your life do you feel you are settling or God wants more for you? Are you willing to improve your active relationships as a father, mother, daughter, brother, husband, or wife? Do you feel that your job has become a meaningless routine, or do you have a purpose in your career? Is it possible that your free time could be used more purposefully, to master a gift, to support a cause, to reach a loss individual, to fulfill a purpose?

As you slowly ingest the words of this book like sipping warm tea, my prayer is that you and God share a spiritual exchange that will change your life forever. I invite you to ask God to help you find the purposeful life you were chosen and called to live.

"For God hath not given us the spirit of fear, but of power, and of love, and of a sound mind." 2 Timothy 1

Allowing the neglect and abuse to go on in a relationship and expecting things to change is one example of how regret grows. Faithfully going to work at the same minimum wage job day in and day out and hoping that you will somehow have a 6-figure income in a year and be able to do more for others is insane unless something about that routine changes. We live in a society where complacency and control kind of pair with each other. We keep doing what we have been doing. It's easy, in routine, and we think we are in control or we can manage. When you come to the understanding, it is ok to be content and grateful but not complacent and that God is in control and we are not your paradigm changes. What am I saying? There is nothing wrong with working a minimum wage job if that is what you desire and are called to do. This book is for those of us who know we are called to a life different than the one we are currently experiencing. We find ourselves satisfied settling for safety, minimal, mediocracy. Then Bow! Life throws a curveball at us. Suddenly the bare minimum is disturbed and we are left feeling like defeated, purposeless, and worthless failures. But God performs miracles in desolate places. The most beneficial relationship you can have is with God, your creator. He is always, beginning, present, and future, looking out for your best interest for his Glory. Building a relationship with God will not only provide you the strength and guidance you seek in all aspects of life including romance, finances and business, but this relationship will open doors made especially for you to live an abundant life scripture and carry God's glory.

"The thief comes only to steal and kill and destroy. I came that they may have life and have it more abundantly" John 10:10

What dreams has God placed on your heart? What desires do you have for your life that will bring God's glory and help others think outside the box? Our creator wants to top whatever you come up with. Boxes are for people who no longer have life, it's time for you to come outside of the box of hopelessness and live a life of your dreams. You do not have to sleep to see your dream in action; your dream can come true and become a reality as it is in heaven right here on earth. If your dream or purpose is to work 30 years at your current job and retire, glory be to God. Whatever your dream is, big or small, God has the best for you and his glory.

Envision yourself 5 years from now and your God-given dream is a reality. God did it for Joseph. Imagine using your passion, talent, and gift to benefit others. Do you have the gift of service, leadership, prophecy, teaching, or encouragement? Can you benefit others through, song, compassion, or art? Are you destined to be a chef, a preacher, a mechanic, or a teacher? Maybe you desire to be an engineer, a director, CEO, an author, philosopher, or scientist. We all have dreams but some of us have given up on bringing them to the past because of the worries of the world. Perhaps you or someone you know has a dream or vision, a goal, something that is special, meaningful, or purposeful living inside of you. Let this be a reminder, the nudge or push to encourage you to change your life. Here is your wakeup call. The only way to make your dreams come true is to act on them. It is time we start living our dreams! There is a better life filled with purpose, peace, and joy. Wake Up!

"We have different gifts, according to the grace given to each of us. If your gift is prophesying, then prophesy in accordance with your faith; if it is serving, then serve; if it is teaching, then teach; if it is to encourage than encourage; if it is giving, then give generously; if it is to lead, do it diligently; if it is to show mercy, do it cheerfully." Romans 12 6-8

"Be not deceived; God is not mocked: for whatsoever a man soweth, that shall he also reap. For he that soweth to his flesh shall reap corruption, but he that soweth to the spirit rea life everlasting. And let us not be weary in well-doing; for in due season we shall reap if we faint not. As we have therefore opportunity, let us do good unto all men, especially unto them who are of the household of faith." Galatians 6:7-10

Dream

What is your dream? What steps are you taking to bring the dream that lives inside of you to the past? Have you set any goals? What have you done to achieve your goal or goals? Is that goal still a goal or is it now "just" a thought, a mere memory, and an idea that never came to reality? Realistically, dreams and goals do change but some just die from neglect, procrastination, fear, or doubt. What is stopping you from pursuing your ideas and using your gift(s)? Is it possible to do what you have dreamed of doing or is it too late? Can you fit it into your busy schedule or is it impossible to make changes? Life is not a dream, but it is the space and time needed to turn a dream into a reality. Dreams do come true but not while we are asleep. It's up to us to turn our dreams into reality with the time we have right now. You wouldn't intentionally waste money so why waste time? I hope you [the readers] find this book to be a form of inspiration, motivation, and guidance as you uncover the beauty of your very meaningful life and to strengthen your relationship with the creator.

"He replied, "If you have faith as small as a mustard seed, you can say unto this sycamine tree, Be thou plucked up by the root, and be though planted in the sea, and it should obey you." Luke 17:6

Action

Goals

Write down a short term and a longterm goal with a date.

Set a daily or weekly time to work on that goal. Set a reminder.

MONDAY	
TUESDAY	
WEDNESDAY	
THURSDAY	
FRIDAY	

Where do you see yourself 5 weeks, 5 months and 5 years from now?

Prayer:

Thank you, God, for your comforting spirit. God, I thank you for the hope I have because of you and the dreams and desires you have placed on my heart. I believe, with you, nothing is impossible. Please help me to grow my faith with works so that you would indeed bless me for your glory.

Time

Time is money right or isn't it? Once time has passed there is no turning back so wake up now and do what you can with the time you have. The saying "time is money" reminds us that time is important! Time well spent makes money and money is important and so is the life we live in. Yet, some of us overlook the fact that time is so much more important than money because you can't replenish it. Time is not tangible or man-made and endless in supply. Our days, although we may not know to what end, are numbered. Without time there would be no need for money. The time we spend working, with others, on our goals and doing nothing at all produce results. Think about it. Forty hours a week creates a paycheck, time spent with others creates a relationship, time spent doing nothing creates the lack thereof. This could mean a lack of stress or a lack of money. Anyone can leave money in a bank account and it will wait, it may even grow. Money can even be multiplied as people lend money and receive more in return by charging interest. You can make a million dollars and spend it and make a million dollars again. It may be much easier to say than to do but the point is, it's possible. The point I am making is that money is tangible, unlimited and it can be manipulated, controlled even. Cash is man-made, and it can be replaced, it can be restored. Money and time can both be invested but can have different kinds of significance. Money comes and goes, but time keeps ongoing. Time waits for no one! Why do we procrastinate? Time and chance happen to us all so why do we decide not to take the chance. Time goes on as we live our lives, start new jobs, go out and party, cook and clean, and as we do nothing. So why not make that time count?

"Do not neglect the spiritual gift you received through the prophecy spoken over you when the elders of the church laid their hands on you." Timothy 4:14

"But, beloved, be not ignorant of this one thing, that one day is with the Lord as a thousand years, and a thousand years as one day." 2 Peter 3:8

Action

Make a schedule designate a set time for devotion, motivation, and working towards your dream

MOTIVATION

Devotion

Working

Prayer:

God, please reveal to me, the gifts you have placed inside me, and the gifts which you have given to me to benefit others and to carry out your will for my life. Thank you for your clarity and understanding. Order my steps so that I may use the gift of time that you have given me wisely. Thank you, father, in Jesus' name.

Procrastination

The idea that the right time will come to "get started" is easy to believe but what does the right time mean? Does it mean that there's a better time ahead that is on its way to us right now? If the right time will come, is now the wrong time? Do you have a lesson to learn before the right time comes? Is there some sort of necessary preparation to complete? Could it be that you are not taking any action at all waiting for the right time because it's the easy road of procrastination? What are you doing in the meantime? It's the present time that means something that matters. When the right time comes, what good is the right time if we are not taking the right actions? There will be times or moments in time when our goal(s) may be easier to carry out and times when they are not. Yet, the time to start to carry out your goal(s) may be sooner rather than later. We must start somewhere.

"For the light makes everything visible. That is why it is said, Awake, O sleeper, rise from the dead, and Christ will give you light. So be careful how you live. Don't live like fools, but like those who are wise. Make the most of every opportunity in these evil days. Don't act thoughtlessly, but understand what the Lord wants you to do." Ephesians 5:14-17

Set a reminder.
Get an accountability partner.
Get to work

Prayer:

Father God, Thank you for the gift of time and the gift of life. I ask for the wisdom and discernment to know the times and the seasons in my life so that I may use my time here on earth wisely. Help me to know when it is time to work and time to rest, time to sow, and time to reap. I pray in Jesus' name, Amen.

Implementation

The time we spend reading produces a message or some sort of education. Children spend time reading and writing to gain insight, to learn vocabulary, to learn skills. Adults spend time in higher learning programs to gain knowledge and earn degrees. We spend time exercising to create better health and to lose weight. We spend time relaxing to create a lack of stress. We spend time caring for others and making memorable moments. We must ask ourselves that are we spending our time in a way that we will look back and appreciate 5, 10, or 20 years from now? I am not saying you should be worried about tomorrow but beneficially using time is a significant part of manifesting visions. Faith without actions is dead. Think about all the time that has passed what knowledge have you gained? What relationships have you developed? What future legacies will you leave?

"Just as the body is dead without breath, so also is faith dead without good works." James 2:26

One of things I've learned is our thoughts and words have much to do with our actions therefore we must think on the things we want to come to past.

"Finally, brothers, whatever is true, whatever is honorable, whatever is just, whatever is pure, whatever is lovely, whatever is commendable, if there is any excellence, if there is anything worthy of praise, think about these things. What you have learned and received and heard and seen in me— practice these things, and the God of peace will be with you."

Philippians 4:8-9 ESV

"The tongue has the power of life and death, and those who love it will eat its fruit."

Proverbs 18:21 NIV

Write 100 Affirmations that you can think on that you plan on manifesting.

Prayer:

Thank you, God, that you are God and I am not. Thank you for trusting and believing in me to use the power of love and self-discipline to live a prosperous and abundant life. When it is time for me to be still, help me to be still, and know that you are God. When is it time for me to work, help me to move with faith and diligence that will move mountains for your glory, in Jesus' name, Amen.

Consider This

What would the world be like today if children didn't go to school because it wasn't the right time, or they chose not to go to school so they could play? Picture two separate children, both age eight, and both residents of Philadelphia, PA. One child has a loving father and mother, older siblings, a big comfy room, plenty of toys, and never wants for anything. Now picture the other eight-year-old child, has a loving single mother, is the oldest of five siblings, shares a room with two siblings, eats based on the meals that his financially challenged mother who is on public services can afford. What do these children have in common other than their age and place of residence? One thing is apparent, they are both loved school-aged and will most likely invest their time in school, they both will invest time in their early childhood education. Is the less fortunate child going to put off going to school because of his mother's financial status, or because of what he ate for dinner? No, these children might go to the same class and receive the same education. Their paths may be different, but their opportunity is the same. Our obstacles may be different from our neighbors, but we still have the ability and chance to succeed. While we are alive and able, we still have the chance to build upon our dreams and ideas.

"Whatever you do, do well. For when you go to the grave, there will be no work or planning or knowledge or wisdom." Ecclesiastes 9:10

Prayer:

God thank you for being a loving God and supplying all my needs to live a purposeful life. Thank you, God, for blessing me with the gifts, talents, and desires of my heart. I pray that you will be done in my life concerning these things so that I may bring you Glory.

Consider This

You may have heard the saying "every penny counts". Well, of course, 100 pennies make a dollar, but if you lose a penny you can get another one, you may even find the same penny you lost. In the same token, "Every minute counts" because there are 60 minutes to every hour. Comparatively, if you lose a minute can it be recovered, will you be able to add another or rewind time? Other than daylight savings time the answer is no. The time that has passed is never coming back. That's just the harsh truth and the truth shall set us free. Now just let that marinate for a second. Our age is determined by the number of minutes, hours, days, and the years we live. Our legacy or memory our footprint, our mark is determined by what we do with that time. From the moment in time of our birth to the moment in time when we take our last breath, every minute counts. Let's imagine everything in life is itemized or recorded like the way merchants or department stores record items or services we purchase using a receipt. A receipt shows the items we bought, the price we paid, the discounts or deductions that apply, and the total. In comparison, our actions are like the items we purchase with time. The way we use our time is a form of farming so to speak. We are farmers of time and the crop or harvest produce is bigger than any word I can use in this context; it is a harvest that not only applies to our life but also our afterlife.

"Even now the one who reaps draws a wage and harvest a crop for eternal life, so that the sower and the reaper may be glad together." John 4:36

Prayer:

Heavenly Father, thank you for the resources including time and money that you have blessed me with and made readily available to me. Please bless with wisdom, understanding, and self-discipline. Help me to use the resources you blessed me with for your will to be done in my life. Help me to yield the best possible results with my time and money for your glory. In Jesus name, Amen

Consider This

The time we spent learning to walk, write, ride a bike, all required a certain amount of time and action. We sowed works and reaped skills. The time we spend sleeping, relaxing, and even eating is like discounts to stress, hunger, exhaustion. You could even say the time we spend doing nothing credits energy, growth, and peace. In comparison, time and money are a lot alike but the permanent effects of wasting the two can be significantly different. Why? Money spent can have less of a permanent effect, primarily because you can usually get a refund if you're not happy with the product or service you purchased. Even with a no refund purchase, you may be able to exchange or resell it. Wasting money is still a bad thing and can cause a significant lack of money and other material things, but you might just have the time to get it back. This may give the false illusion that money is more useful than time but when you die, you can't take it with you. Time works differently and to take advantage of the time we have left we must be conscious diligent and proactive. Unfortunately, there is no stopping the clock, you can't get the time you've spent back. However, on the bright side, the good news is you are reading this book, it is not too late, and you are not out of time. What are you buying with your time this year or this week or even just today? Are you procuring something meaningful? Are you spending your time on something that will have been beneficial in your afterlife 20 years from now, tomorrow, or today? Are you storing up riches for your afterlife? We must be mindful of our time used, planned, and spent because it will count or discount for something. You wouldn't take your money and just waste it, so why do we waste our time as if it is expendable?

"Let's not get tired of doing what is good, for at the right time we will reap a harvest if we do not give up" Galatians 6:9

Prayer:

Thank you, God, for strength. Father, please help me to be consistent even in times of weariness so that I may reap the benefits you have stored up for me in due season. Your word says no weapon formed against me shall prosper, thank you for protecting me from all weapons in the spiritual and natural, in Jesus name, Amen.

Consider This

Somedays, I would just lie in bed doing nothing and there is nothing wrong with doing so, but there can be a thin line between relaxing and wasting time. Although resting is a part of life, the thought crossed my mind to use my time more wisely. I needed to use more of my time investing in growth and things that contribute to a better me. It is important to have a rest day but be mindful not to rest so much you lose sight of growing. Dedicating time to my beliefs was one way I decided to use my rest time more wisely. One of the devotionals I read mentioned a quote from Thomas Edison which read "Time is the only capital that any human being has, and the only thing he can't afford to lose". This is wisdom that is vital on so many different levels and yet it goes over the heads of many people. I mean, how many people like to live in the moment as if tomorrow doesn't exist? Lots of people, right? I am guilty of this too. I have been there and done that. I have had weeks, months even, when I didn't even think about yesterday or tomorrow let alone investing time in the present. Guess what, time didn't pause just because I did.

"Don't let anyone look down on you because you are young, but set an example for the believers in speech, in conduct, in love, in faith, and in purity." 1Timothy 4: 12

Prayer:

Thank you, heavenly father, for being a faithful and just God. Please help me to see your will for my life beyond my past mistakes, beyond my natural limitations and the opinions of others. Help me to use my youth for your glory and not as a time to waste in Jesus' name, Amen.

Consider This

How many people are stuck today because they are focused on the past or busy trying to just live in the moment? Too many people. Sometimes it is not only ok but important to let your hair down, live in the moment but only for a moment. The truth is it is all about balance. What is your life centered around? Is it money, food, material things, attention, or God? There are those of us who have been doing the same useless, unprofitable, ruinous things for years and just avoiding the significant details of our life actions. Of course, I'm not saying not to enjoy the moment but so many of us live and stay in the moment as if we don't have an expiration date. Some of us are simply trying to survive. Then there are those of us who live in the pain and regrets of the past as if today isn't a new day filled with new opportunities and new experiences. Opposingly, there are those people who have invested a significant amount of time in prosperous, purposeful, or memorable things. Some of us are doing well at investing in all three but still missing a healthy balance. A healthy balance will consist of more investing, creating, and doing with less wasting, slumbering, and procrastinating.

"Whoever sows sparingly will also reap sparingly, and whoever sows bountifully will also reap bountifully." 2 Corinthians 9:6

"But seek ye first the kingdom of God and his righteousness, and all these things shall be added unto you." Matthew 6: 33

Prayer:

Dear God, thank you for your living word that is forever constantly working in me and my life. Father, please help me to focus on you and to hear your voice above all else. Help me to begin and maintain a healthy balanced God-centered life mentally, physically, and spiritually. I thank you father for the fruits of the spirit and the fruits of my obedience to your word, in Jesus' name, Amen.

Consider This

Who is perfect? I certainly am not and truth be told, nobody is. I am the last to judge you, but does that mean you shouldn't live your best life? Are you honestly happy with yourself and the person you are today? Do you find yourself ponder your actions with regret? It's not too late to start making decisions you won't regret it. Do you search for yourself and critic yourself? If not, then you may want to start. However, you do not have the right to condemn yourself. It is extremely important that we do self-assessments' because we are our own best critics. It is important that we acknowledge where we are so that we can set goals and expectations for where we would like to be. Although we are our own best critics, some of us are also in denial about the improvements we need to make. Think of something you wanted to do one or maybe even two years ago. Maybe you wanted to write a book, go to college, quit a bad habit, pay off some debt, write a song, end a bad relationship, start a good relationship, apologize and ask for forgiveness, give someone else forgiveness or do something else meaningful to you. Maybe you want to make amends or accept Jesus Christ as your Lord and savior. While God is merciful with time we should not put off what we can do today. We are only getting older and time is only going forward.

"I returned, and saw under the sun, that the race is not to the swift, nor the battle to the strong, neither yet bread to the wise, nor riches to men of understanding, nor favor to men of skill; but time and chance happeneth to them all." Ecclesiastes 9:11

"But the Lord said to me, "Do not say, 'I am too young.' You must go to everyone I send you to and say whatever I command you." Jeremiah 1:7

Prayer:

Dear Father and Friend, Thank you for the favor of my life. Thank you for your grace and mercy that is renewed every day. Please help me to make the most of today, tomorrow, and the days to come, living my very best life for your glory. I pray in Jesus' name, Amen.

Consider This

Today is the day to start holding yourself accountable! Make your time count for something! Tomorrow is going to come rather you are here to witness it or not! Ask yourself am I doing all that I possibly can do to turn my dreams into reality? If so, then kudos to you! You are doing the right thing by sewing or investing time into bettering yourself, achieving your goals, improving your quality of life, and being whomever God created you to be. Be grateful, give God the Glory! Even if you do not get the results you want right away, at least you are working on success and your day will come. You are already on your way to living your best life! Now, if you feel that the results you have are not a true testament of your efforts maybe it is time to re-evaluate. Is there a lesson to be learned? Is there an easier or more appropriate way to achieve your goal? Is it meditation, prayer, or patience that you need? Is it a matter of learning diligence and discipline? Those of you reading this who are not doing all that you can to achieve your goal, what are you waiting for? Seriously, think about it, what is the hold-up? Is it the motivation you need? Is it the support you need? Is negativity holding you back? Is it all mental or in your mind? What is stopping you from taking ten to thirty minutes a day or more to do what you want to do? Maybe it is nobody but you and your thoughts. Pick up a pen and write that poem, song, or book! Pick up a paintbrush and go paint! Go to the gym and exercise!

"For we live by faith, not by sight." 2 Corinthians 5:7

"I had fainted unless I had seen the goodness of the Lord in the land of the living. Wait on the Lord: be of good courage, and he shall strengthen thine heart: wait I say on the Lord." Psalm 27:14

Prayer:

Dear heavenly Father, I thank you for supplying all my needs. Help me see that this is evident in my time of need. Renew my mind and pour out your spirit in me so that I may live in faith and do that which you have given me the power to do. Thank you for your spirit of power love and self-discipline. Thank you that today I am more than a conqueror, in Jesus' name, Amen.

Consider This

Are you waiting for money? Or is money waiting for you? The lack of money can be a hindrance if you let it to be. Many times, money is an easy answer but not the only answer. In the times you feel the money would make a difference it is time to be resourceful. Think outside the box? What can you do with what you have? Can you network by using your spare time to volunteer to help others for a cause you believe in if not one that is related to what you want to achieve? Maybe you can just start somewhere in your free time for example like writing a budget plan, going to a finance class, writing music, exercising at home? Could you share your gift or passion simply by using social media? Time is a gift and it is up to you to use it to make a difference. It's ok to enjoy the moment because you're never going to relive that very same moment but be careful of your time not to waste it. Y.O.L.O. (you on live once).

"And my God shall supply all your needs according to his riches and glory in Christ Jesus" Philippians 4:19

Prayer:

Dear heavenly father, I am so blessed to be your child. I am grateful that I have more than enough. Help me to talk to the appointed people at the appointed time to bring plans you have put on my heart to the past. Help me to utilize the resources you have provided me to the fullest potential just as you did with five loaves of bread and two fish. Thank you, dear lord, in Jesus› name.

Consider This

You don't get another life... So, let the past be the past, enjoy the present but live for a better future. Considering you don't get a do-over, and considering time waits for no one you probably want to make this your best life. In other words, you should want to be the best you that you can be starting now! The only person that can't stop you from being whom you want to be is you! Make your past self envious of you now and your present-self jealous of the future you! No one can stand in your way more than yourself. Similarly, no one can cause you to be great more than yourself.

"Therefore, if anyone is in Christ, the new creation has come: the old has gone, the new is here!" 2 Corinthians 5: 17

Exercising on the treadmill, at planet fitness, I looked down at the treadmill and saw the PF slogan "No Critics". Although many of us have critics that care about us and truly love us, such as parents, siblings, significant other friends, we don't always appreciate constructive criticism. There are also those critics that leave a bad taste in the mouth also known as foes, haters, and some are random people who are just brutally and boldly rude and offensive. Sad to say, but some people are content verbally abusing people without thought are regard to emotions. We all have people around us who are straight shooters and then those who will sugar coat their message. Either way, sometimes the truth is a really hard pill to swallow. You can probably think of a moment in the past when someone said something you felt was harmful, harsh, or just none of their business. Well, it's time to wake up self-examine, self-criticize, and self-reflect, regardless of how they see us we are our own best critics. We owe it to ourselves, to be honest with ourselves about what we can do better. The person dishing criticism may have no idea what hardships you're dealing with right now but there may be some truth in what they are saying. In reality, is it's your job to take that negative energy and make it something positive.

"Love your enemies and pray for those who persecute you." Matthew 5:44

"Do not judge others, and you will not be judged. For you will be treated as you treat others. The standard you use in judging is the standard by which you will be judged." Matthew 7:1-2

"Why do you look at the speck of sawdust in your brother's eye and pay no attention to the plank in your own eye? How can you say to your brother, 'Brother, let me take the speck out of your eye,' when you yourself fail to see the plank in your own eye, and then you will see clearly to remove the

speck from your brother's eye." Luke 6: 41, 42

Prayer:

God, thank you, that you are God and I am not. Help me to see the error of my ways so that I may correct them. Help me to be whom you called me to be. Your word states that I am a child of God. Help me to act more like you and to think more like you. Help me be quick to listen, slow to anger, and slow to speak. In Jesus' name, I pray, Amen.

Consider This

We are not obligated to live our best life, to be the best we can be, or to use our gifts and talents but not to be the greatest disservice that we can render ourselves. Life is 10% of what happens and 90% of how we deal with it. You hold the key to your success; you hold the power to your change, and this is your life and your story! A key is no good unless one uses it to unlock the door to which it opens. Your attention will determine your direction. Your actions will demand results. Your attitude will determine your future. Most importantly your time spent will define you as a person. Wake up and do what you really want to do! Your life is a book and time is your pencil write what you will!

"After a long time, their master returned from his trip and called them to give an account of how they had used his money. The servant to whom he had entrusted the five bags of silver came forward with five more bags of silver to invest, and I have earned five more. The Master was full of praise. Well done, my good and faithful servant. You have been faithful in handling this small amount, so now I will give you many more responsibilities. Let's celebrate together." Matthew 25: 19-20

Make a list of people who you have wronged ask the father to forgive you and the person if possible. Make a list of people have wronged you and ask for God to heal you from any pain it may have cause. Pray for them! Who can you love today?

Love

Do you love what you do? Does what you do positively affect others? Do you have peace of mind from what you do? Do you feel warm and fuzzy inside as a result when you go to sleep at night? Do you feel you are fulfilling your purpose in life? Does what you do make you happy? I sure hope so because Love is the lack of stress! Love is the lack of fear! Love is the lack of doubt and pain! Love is the rewarding abundance of peace that you get when you have used your time wisely and effectively and you know it is because you can feel the peace and joy that abounds in love. Love is the remedy to sadness. Love is the tingling feeling that you get when you have overflowing joy. Love is so strong and powerful that it is contagious, it trickles over and spills over on the people around you.

"There is no fear in love; but perfect love casteth out fear: because fear hath torment. He that feareth is not made perfect in love" 1 John 4:18

Prayer:

Dear Father, Help me to embody the Agape love you give to me. Help me to love others as I love myself. Let me be filled with your perfect love and wisdom and free of all fear. In Jesus' name, Amen.

Love is light without darkness. Love is a feeling no drug or alcohol can surpass. Love is the chills you get when someone's positive energy trickles over and overwhelms you! Love is bright enough to kick out darkness. Love is the absence of negativity. Love is the absence of hate! Love is the purest form of water the soul can taste. Love is an action and a feeling, an emotion, and a verb. You deserve love. You deserve to receive it, to feel it, to give it, and to rest in it. Love is the only thing more powerful than time! Do you have love? Do you really, I mean really have love? If you can't say yes, it's time to self-reflect. Your love should not depend on any other human being past or present. Love is not something that can be limited. In fact, love is the only thing we can give and receive without any measure.

"And the light shineth in darkness; and the darkness comprehended it not."
John 1:5

Prayer:

God, thank you, for being all the light that I need in the midst of darkness. Please help me to shine your light and to be a powerful example to those who are fighting the darkness for your glory. I pray in Jesus' name, Amen.

To love is the only way to be truly free and limitless. The lack of love comes with unnecessary weight. Love is limitless and does not require compensation. Love doesn't cost a thing if it's given and received sincerely! If you don't have love wake up because you are truly missing out on one of life's greatest gifts. Get you some love because there is plenty to go around since love's true love is endless. If you have love, share the love, spread the love, and grow the love! It will only make you happier and strengthen your love.

"Jesus said unto him, Thou shalt love the Lord thy God with all thy heart, and with all thy soul, and with all thy mind. This is the first commandment. And the second is like, unto it, Thou shalt love thy neighbor as thyself."
Matthew 22: 37-39

Prayer:

God please heal my heart of stone and give me a heart of flesh. Pour out your power in love that it may run over and flow through me to those I encounter. Thank you, Father, in Jesus' name, Amen.

When is the last time you smiled? When is the last time you were the reason someone else smiled? When is the last time you felt giddy inside? That was love and we all deserve it, so share it with someone. You will feel good when you do... There will be times when you will love, and you will feel like the love you gave was not appreciated or reciprocated. You will wonder why. You may even feel hurt, abused, misused, neglected, and mistreated. You will want to take your love back. Do not let that rub off on you or negatively affect the way you love. That person that didn't appreciate your love is probably going through something... or not. He or she may be dealing with the lack of self-love or an abundance of negativity. Your ability to love should not depend on others. Your love doesn't run out, you are filled with love from the creator! Love is a flower planted that grows without end, it is a crop that cannot be swept away with the wind, devoured by a pest, or lost in a storm. Love is invincible. It cost us nothing to love each other. When you share your love and it is not reciprocated it is because that other being needed that love more than you expected. Not everyone knows or understands the true power of love. Don't worry, your love comes from an endless and unconditional supply, you can give more love and you must.

"And to love him with all the heart, and with all the understanding, and with all the soul, and with all the strength, and to love his neighbour as himself, is more than all whole burnt offerings and sacrifices." Mark 12:33

Prayer:

Dear Father, create in me a clean heart and renew a right spirit in me. Help me not to be spiritually or emotionally harmed by the ways of the people around me. Soften the heart of those who persecute me and bless those who want to harm me with new hearts filled with your love. I pray in Jesus' name, Amen.

Guard your heart when you love so that negativity does not sneak in while you let love flow out. Love without expectation, disappointment, and hurt is not an option. Love is invincible, but our hearts are not. Protect your peace and heart by all means but do not allow someone else's negativity to cause you to be negative or to stop loving. Loving God is just as important as loving others so don't confuse sharing love with giving up your peace or accepting abuse. Love does not have to be painful. Sometimes we forget how to love and so do the people that we share our love with. Sometimes we let pain, anger, fear, regret, and negativity in, and our love machine stops producing and goes on standby. In order to understand how to love, we have to understand God's love for us. Do not allow the past or actions of others to block your flow of love. Chances are if you stop loving you will start doing the opposite which will only lead to regret. Your peace and ability to love should never depend on another person. It is your job to know your self-worth and rid yourself of negativity.

"Guard your heart above all else, for it determines the course of your life."
Proverbs 4:23

Prayer:

Dear Heavenly Father, I thank you for your living word which states that no weapon formed against me shall prosper. Help me to guard my heart with your love and the peace that surpasses all understanding. I pray in Jesus' name, Amen.

The reality is, there will be many moments in your life when you are putting out love and you are not getting the same love in return. It can feel like you are being sucked dry like you are running out of love, but you are in a spiritual war between love and fear, peace and chaos, good and evil. The enemy wants to steal your joy by using others to stir emotions that can steal time, peace, and prosperity. You are expecting others to love you in a way only God can love you. You owe it yourself to put distance and space between yourself and that kind of energy. Sometimes you will have to love people from afar. Pray for those whom you feel are against you. Hold your peace and watch God's move.

"But I say unto you, Love your enemies, bless them that curse you, do good to them that hate you, and pray for them which despitefully use you."

Prayer:

Dear God, I ask you to be my strong tower and my place of refuge when others conspire against me or try to harm me. Protect me from the snares of my enemies. Bless them with the fear of the lord, forgiveness, love, and peace, in Jesus' name I pray, Amen.

Having a forgiving heart, keeping your peace, and moving on to the love you deserve is healthy and an important part of understanding God's love for us and in us. A friend of mine told me that it was nice to be around me because it was like I entered their peace and there were no ripples. When you skip a rock in a pond of water it creates ripples. This is called the ripple effect. The rock is foreign energy that hits the water and creates ripples, movement, and change in the energy of the pond. In life, people will throw rocks in our water intentionally and unintentionally. Unlike a pond, we can control whom we surround ourselves with. Words and actions can both be seen as ripples. In life, these ripples can be positive energy or negative energy. It is up to you to pay attention because people can only do to you what you allow them to do to you. Your heart is the key to your peace so protect your heart by keeping your trust in God and not in man. Surround yourself with others who love to love and who also strive to understand what it is to strive to love like God.

"Then came Peter to him, and said, Lord, how oft shall my brother sin against me, and I forgive him? till seven times? Jesus saith unto him, I say not unto thee, Until seven times; but, Until seventy times seven." Matthew 18:21-22

"Blessed is the one who does not walk in step with the wicked or stand in the way that sinners take or sit in the company of mockers," Psalm 1:1

Dear father, let you will be done in my life. Place the right people and connections in my life for your glory. Help me to maintain a forgiving heart but not to make foolish decisions by surrounding myself with the wrong people. Please surround me with the people who are for me and not against me in Jesus name I pray, Amen.

Self-worth is extremely important. If you don't already know your worth, it is time you do. Look in the mirror and say to yourself "I am fearfully and wonderfully made!" You were made in the womb and planted by God.

Your purpose was known before your parents even met. Your creator does not make mistakes, he makes masterpieces. You are a MASTERPIECE! Affirm to yourself "I am God's masterpiece, I am whom God says I am no matter who loves me he loves me. I will not allow the negative energy or idea of me to interfere with the self-worth God himself has given me. I am special because there is only one me. I am beautiful because love is beautiful, and love lives inside me. I will not allow the negative energy from others to disrupt my peace or poison my heart. Love is endless, so I will love God and I will love others as I love myself. I will share my love without harming myself." You are loved even if you are the only person in your close circle exuding love.

"For thou hast possed my reins: thou hast covered me in my mother's womb. I will praise thee; for I am fearfully and wonderfully made: marvelous are thy works; and that my soul knoweth right well." Psalm 139: 13-14

God sent him to buy freedom for us who were slaves to the law so that he could adopt us as his very own children. And because we are his children, God has sent the spirit of his Son into our hearts, prompting us to call out, Abba, Father. Now you are no longer a slave but God's own child. And since you are his child, God has made you an heir." Galatians 4:5-7

Love is like a light and even the smallest light will shine in the darkness. Love is a choice, so choose to love others as you love yourself. Some people believe that time heals all wounds. As time keeps on going and magically moves the negative energy, we call pain, from our lives. I believe time unquestionably helps in the healing process, but that love is the main ingredient in that healing process. Pain is associated with fear. You may be able to recall a time when you were younger, or when your child was hurt, and a kiss made it all better. As human beings, we crave and require love and affection. We crave God's love, the love of others and to give love. We owe it to ourselves not only to accept and acknowledge God's love for us but also to share that love with others. You reap what you sow and when we sow love, it grows. When you sow in tears you reap joy.

"You are the light of the world. A town built on a hill can bot be hidden. Neither do people light a lamp and put it under a bowl. Instead, they put it on its stand, and it gives light to everyone in the house." Matthew 5: 14-15

"Whoever does not love does not know God, because God is love." 1 John 4:8

Be careful not to confuse love and affection with lust or weakness. Loving should not put you in harm's way. If you are doing something that you believe is exuding love but it's harmful or dangerous you should ask yourself, is this foolish? You do not have to be a fool to love. You do not have to harm yourself to give love or to be loved. Sometimes in life and love, we will make sacrifices, but it is important to know when to draw the line. If a sacrifice is harming your mental or physical health or even causing you to deal with unnecessary pain and strife, chances are you are making a foolish sacrifice. You may even be making a foolish sacrifice out of love, but you must weigh the damage. Now, this does not mean there will not be trying times in love or that you want to have to exercise patience because you will. If your sacrifice is pleasurable to another but harmful to yourself, you need to think about why it is that you are doing it. Do you want gratification, attention, love, approval, affection, kudos, or something from the person for which you are making a sacrifice? I can't tell you how to feel or whom to serve but I can tell you anyone who wants you to suffer doesn't deserve your sacrifice.

"Love is patient, love is kind. It does not boast, it is not proud. It does not dishonor others, it is not self-seeking, it is not easily angered, it keeps no record of wrongs. Love does not delight in evil but rejoices with the truth. It always protects, always trusts, always hope, always perseveres." 1 Corinthians 13:4-6

"No one lights a lamp and puts it in a place where it will be hidden, or under a bowl. Instead, they put it on its stand, so that those who come in may see the light. Your eye is the lamp of your body. When your eyes are healthy, your whole body also is full of light. But when they are unhealthy, your body also is full of darkness. See to it, then, that the light within you is not darkness. Therefore, if your whole body is full of light, and no part of it dark, it will be just as full of light as when a lamp shines its light on you." Luke 11: 33-36

Maybe you feel like the things you've done, or events of your past makes you undeserving. Maybe you are holding onto guilt from something you did in the past. Why is that you haven't forgiven yourself and asked for forgiveness? What is stopping you from forgiving yourself? If you are so terrible than how are you able to love someone else? If you are so undeserving why do you think a sacrifice will help? If you are so unworthy, why are there people who have done what you have done or worse who still experience peace and love? The reason is that you are only as worthy or as deserving as you believe you are. I am not saying you should be content with doing wrong or hurting others, but you must move on, change your mindset, and accept forgiveness. Guilt will rob you of love and peace. If you don't believe you are capable of being loved why should anyone else?

If you don't think you are worthy of being loved why should anyone else? Your attention will determine your direction. Your actions will demand results. The way you think and your attitude, which will determine your future. So, if this is about you it is time to forgive yourself. You can't take back whatever it is that you did but you can ask for forgiveness. You can't change your past, but you can regroup, redirect, and build your future. You can't change who you were, but you can choose who you are now. Forgive yourself and make a conscious decision not to do "it" whatever "it" is again.

"For as he thinketh in his heart, so is he: Eat and drink, saith he to thee; but his heart is not with thee." Proverbs 23: 7

"For all have sinned, and come short of the glory of God;" Romans 3: 23

Sacrifices aren't always pleasant, and they usually consist of giving up something meaningful to us to help another person. Sacrifices can be good and can initiate results. God loves a cheerful giver, however, a foolish sacrifice will bring about foolish results. Instead of making a foolish sacrifice try helping others in a way that doesn't harm you. God's perfect will is made perfect in you when you are obedient. Is your sacrifice in obedience with God? As long as you are alive you can decide whom you want to be. You choose what sacrifices you make. You can decide how much unnecessary pain you choose to deal with. If you are making a continuous sacrifice that is causing you pain or strife it may be in vain. Everyone or everything is not worth that kind of sacrifice so make sure you are wise with your sacrifices. There is a big difference between sacrificing spending money for a savings goal or to give to a bigger cause and using your rent or bill money to impress someone. Likewise, there is a difference between sacrificing your leisure time to help others who are in need or volunteering for a good cause and missing work or "me time" to please someone who could care less about your well-being let alone your goals. Remember that your happiness doesn't come from others, it starts within you. In order to be happy you need to know that you are forgiven and indebted to no one. Be secure in your love. Be careful not to overextend yourself and not to make harmful sacrifices.

"Being justified freely by his grace through the redemption that is in Christ Jesus: Whom God hath set forth to be a propitiation through faith in his blood, to declare his righteousness for the remission of sins that are past, through the forbearance of God;" Romans 3: 24-25

"Behold, I send you forth as sheep in the midst of wolves: be ye wise as a serpent, and harmless as doves." Matthew 10: 16

All of us have people around us who shed love on us. Pay attention to the people who support your dreams, have positive things to say, and encourage you to be happy. Remember they can't supply you love and peace but they can add to it. Show your appreciation and do not take these kinds of people for granted. We can become a product of our environment, so we should choose our environment accordingly. When we surround ourselves with negative, ruinous, and miserable people, it is harder to keep the negativity out. Likewise, when we surround ourselves with people who are positive, loving, and peaceful, it is easier to let love in and out. Furthermore, when we surround ourselves with likeminded people it is easier to do what we love. So, what is it that you like to do or dream of doing? Maybe you like to sing, dance, write, draw, paint, build, act, read, or maybe you are more into sports, math, or science. There is something inside of you waiting to grow if not to be born in the first place. That love, that gift, that purpose is worth your attention. Do not allow excuses or doubt to rob you of your joy. Do not be like those who would stay asleep in their life rather than live life awake. I'm too old they say, I'm too busy they say, I have nothing to offer they say as if the very air they breathe is worthless.

"Beware of false prophets, which come to you in sheep's clothing, but inwardly they are ravening wolves. Yes, shall know them by their fruits. Do men gather grapes of thorns or figs of thistles? Even so, every good tree bringeth forth good fruit; but a corrupt tree bringeth forth evil fruit."
Matthew 17: 15-20

"Blessed is the man that walketh not in the counsel of the ungodly, nor standeth in the way of sinners, nor sitteth in the seat of the scornful. But his delight is in the Lord; and he meditates day and night. And he shall be like a tree planted by the rivers of water, that bringeth forth his fruit in his season; his leaf also shall not wither, and whatsoever he doth shall prosper."
Psalm 1: 1-3

The only way to win is to try. Making the conscious decision of not trying is the easiest way to fail. Challenge yourself to try. If you have physical or monetary limitations, think about how you can work around them. Use the resources you have so that the resources you need might be added. There is no perfect blueprint or specific route to success, love, and peace other than the word of God. Everyone takes different paths, avenues, and ways to achieve their dreams but keep a positive, willing, and loving attitude. Your actions will demand results. Your attention will determine your direction. Your attitude will determine your future. Most importantly your time spent will define you as a person. Stay away from the naysayer. Surround yourself with positive-minded people who know how to love.

"Delight they self also in the Lord and he shall give thee the desires of thine heart.' Psalms 37: 4

"The plans of the diligent lead to profit as surely as haste leads to poverty." Proverbs 21; 5

" Blessed is the man that walketh not in the counsel of the ungodly, nor standeth in the way of sinners, nor sitteth in the seat of the scornful" Psalm 1:1

Write 5 things you will do this week to
improve your overall health.

42

Health

What is health for you? Is health about how many meals you eat a day, exercise, or lack of stress? There are so many factors that contribute to our health mentally, physically, and even spiritually. To be healthy is a state of mental, physical, and spiritual well-being. Are you living your best life? Are you living a healthy lifestyle? Unhealthy living can be an addictive, easy, and lazy regiment of bad decisions and significantly harmful to our well-being. Most people picture an unhealthy lifestyle as eating a big fat cheese whiz bacon stacked beef burger, days of being slumped over on the couch, smoking, and drinking like every day is a celebration. Either this sounds like tons of fun to you or terribly unhealthy which depends on you and your perspective! Either way, I can agree, this sounds like a heart attack waiting to happen but also a fun time for some people. Some people live this kind of lifestyle and at the doctor's office their vital signs, blood pressure, and health screening tests show no signs of illness as if they were doing something right. Other people eat so carefully that you couldn't imagine any type of disease or illness reaching them with a 10-foot pole and suddenly they're diagnosed with cancer. It's almost as if health is like a roll of the dice. Why is it that it seems unhealthy habits will catch up with some people and not others? Is it grace? Is there more to health than just fruits, grain, veggies, and exercise? Does it have to do with spirituality? What can we do differently to be a healthier us?

"He gives strength to the weary and increases the power of the weak. Even youths grow tired and weary and young men stumble and fall, but those who hope in the Lord will renew their strength. They will soar on wings like eagles; they will run and not grow weary, they will walk and not be faint."
Isaiah 40: 29-31

"Honor your father and your mother, so that you may live long in the Land of the Lord your God is giving you." Exodus 20:12

Sometimes our unhealthy decisions can be more obscure like talking to the wrong people who bring negative energy. Sometimes the stress and negativity can cause health issues. It is vital for us to be able to live and move in peace. More importantly is it imperative that we be in control of our peace. Letting the people that you interact with, on a day to day or random basis, steal your joy is not ok. Negativity can be like a cloud that hovers above us. In the midst of negativity, we have to be prepared to weather the storm. You have to carry your umbrella to shield yourself from bad vibes, put on your rain boots to walk through it, and of course, wear your raincoat so that you can protect your body from the bad weather. The sun will shine again. Protecting your peace of mind and your health is vital to being happy and healthy. We don't have a meteorologist, or weatherman to tell us what kind of obstacles we will deal with every day but that doesn't mean we can't be prepared. We also need to treat our bodies the way we do anything else we care for. For some of us, this means eating healthier or even exercising more. Maybe you have children that you care deeply about, or a pet, or a home, or even a car. When you care about something passionately you want to give it your best. You want to nurture, protect, and preserve it. You also deserve your best. Do the same with your mind body and spirit. Y.O.L.O. Nurture your spirit with positive, love, peace, joy, forgiveness, laughter, and wisdom. Nurture your mind with education, good thoughts, good music, and plans for tomorrow. Nurture your body with nutritious foods, exercise, rest, and wellness.

"For our struggle is not against flesh and blood, but against the rulers, against authorities, against the powers of this dark world and spiritual forces of evil in the heavenly realms. Therefore put on the full armor of God, so that when the day of evil comes you may be able to stand your ground, and after you have done everything, to stand. Stand firm then, with the belt of truth buckled around your waist, with the breastplate of righteousness in place, and with your feet fitted with the readiness that comes from the gospel of peace. In addition to all this, take up the shield of faith, with which you can extinguish all the flaming arrows of the evil one. Take the helmet of salvation and the sword of the spirit which is the word of God."
Ephesians 6:12-17

"The human spirit can endure in sickness, but a crushed spirit who can bear? The heart of the discerning acquires knowledge, for the ears of the wise seek it out." Proverbs 18: 14-15

The body is not a gift you can return if you don't like it. Your body is not replaceable. Although in this present time you can cut and add to your physical appearances we still can't replace the whole body itself. Our body is the home to our soul and we only get one. Exercise is not only good for the body but also for the soul. You wouldn't let your home pile up excess filth, you wouldn't fill it with lots of trash and I hope that you wouldn't let poisonous hazards in your home. So why do we do this with our bodies? Exercise and good nutrition for our bodies are like cleaning and maintenance for our homes. "Physical fitness is not only one of the most important keys to a healthy body, it is the basis of dynamic and creative intellectual activity" John F. Kennedy. "We are all human beings, and we all have insecurities, but it's about being healthy and happy with yourself. I'm not perfect, and I will indulge in pizza and sweets on occasion. The goal is to make the majority of your decisions good for your body. So, listen to your body, and treat it like your temple." Jacqueline Macinnes Wood. True enjoyment comes from the activity of the mind and exercise of the body; the two are ever united." Wilhelm von Humboldt.

"Or do you not know that your body is the temple of the Holy Spirit who is in you, whom you have from God and you are not your own? For you were bought at a price; therefore glorify God in your body and in your spirit which is God's." 1 Corinthians 6: 19-20

"Likewise you also, reckon yourselves to be dead indeed to sin, but alive to God in Christ Jesus our Lord. Therefore do not let sin reign in your mortal body, that you should obey it in its lusts. And do not present your members as instruments of righteousness to God. For sin shall not have dominion over you, for you are not under law but under grace." Romans 6:11-14

If you could for a moment step outside of your body and carry it around like it were a separate entity you might appreciate it more. You may even take more time out to consider the many ways you can make beneficial or healthier choices. Some of us treat our possessions better than we treat our own bodies. Genesis 1:29 reads "And God said, Behold, I have given you every herb bearing seed, which [is] upon the face of all the earth, and every tree, in which [is] the fruit of a tree yielding seed; to you, it shall be for meat." God provides all sorts of fruits, herbs, and vegetables for us to enjoy. Although God first intended more of a vegan and vegetarian diet for us he gave us the freedom to choose. Genesis 9:3 reads "Every moving thing that liveth shall be meant for you; even as the green herb have I given you all things." While God created food in a way that we can enjoy and indulge food is created to sustain our bodies nutritionally. Life is about balance and order. It is important that we discern what is right and what is excessive. Your body is the home to your spirit and soul so cherish it. Mental and Spiritual health is just as important as physical health. Some helpful ways you can improve your overall health include meditation and yoga. Wellness visits are also a major part of health consider talking to your doctor if you have questions or concerns. It's ok to feel shy but the only way to work on your mental health is to talk about it.

There was no life manual that I was introduced to before I was born. Even as I grew into an adult, my instructions were few and my mind was curious. Some of us have excellent mentors and teachers in our lives and some of us do not. Even still we are all capable of making the same mistakes and the same progressive achievements. We can do whatever we choose to put our mind body and spirit to. There is no telling how easy or how hard it will be. I can't give you a timeline on how long it will take you to lose weight or find love, but I can tell you the difference between someone who has made progress and some who hasn't is the fact that one gave up mentally, physically, and possibly even spiritually. A Healthy mind leads to healthy choices. If you feel depressed all the time, suicidal, super happy and super sad, lifeless work on getting help. Spiritual and mental health is important, so I recommend seeking help for both. Too often we let our pride get in the way of our growth. Whether you need to be honest with yourself about the bad habits you should shake or stop being in denial about areas where you need improvement, you first must admit your own faults to yourself. People are going to laugh and talk about you. People will even scold you and criticize you to your face. Turn the pain into motivation. It's ok to swallow your pride. It is important to humble yourself to grow. At some point, you will decide to continue repeating your old childish ways or to start making better decisions. There are so many actions you can take such as a fast, a cleanse or even making a nutritional lifestyle change.

"Do not conform to the pattern of this world, but be transformed by the renewing of your mind. Then you will be able to test and approve what God's will is his good, pleasing, and perfect will." Romans 12:2

Spiritual Growth

Some of us are not in sync with our spirit, our inner being. Religion is often mistaken for spirituality. Religion is a guideline or a belief system to some, but spirituality is bigger than rules and traditions practiced by man. I believe that Jesus Christ is the Son of God who died and rose again to free humanity from sin, condemnation, and eternal death. However, it is the principles and spiritual growth that I value most about my beliefs. I value the fruits of the spirit forgiveness, love, patience, gentleness, and self-control. I feel so much more at peace and in control, content even, when I have my emotions in check. The weight of fear, anger, regret, pain, hate, ill will can all be so heavy to carry around. Hanging on to the negativity of the past is not worth the energy it takes from one's happiness. Worrying and stressing about things that we have no control over has no benefit but instead only brings about a lack of peace. You owe it to yourself, your family, and friends to be spiritually balanced. The spiritual balance will positively impact the way you see your life. Additionally, spirituality has been known to encourage well-being and even improve mental, physical, and emotional health overall.

"But the fruit of the Spirit is love, joy, peace, forbearance, kindness, goodness, faithfulness, 23 gentlenesses, and self-control. Against such things, there is no law." Galatians 5: 22-23

There is something about knowing and giving into that higher power that is liberating and lightening. You do not have to carry around the weight of the past regrets, mistakes, or disappointments. You gain the opportunity and ability to find a surreal peace and understanding which is absent when there is a lack of spiritual well-being. You get to be free and born again. The physical laws that abound us are an "eye for an eye" and a "tooth for a tooth". People believe they should treat people how people treat them, instead of treating people how they would like to be treated. The laws around us do not talk about forgiveness but vengeance. If you hate me I must hate you back. We live in a world where our past shortcomings define who we are, and our old habits are not forgotten even after we change or overcome. When you are enlightened spiritually such laws no longer control or dictate your actions, expectations, and beliefs. Someone who is not spiritually growing may have the "I'll never be anything more than what I was" mentality.

"Take my yoke upon you, and learn of me; for I am meek and lowly in heart, and ye shall find rest unto your souls. For my yoke is easy and my burden is light." Matthew 11:29-30

"Dearly beloved, avenge not yourselves, but rather give place unto wrath: for it is written, Vengeance is mine; I will repay, saith the Lord." Romans 12;19

Change is constant and in change lies growth. It is important that you allow yourself to grow and change regardless of your past regrets. We are not born experienced geniuses with life all figured out. Instead, we are born without the knowledge of how to eat, talk, crawl, and walk. One thing we are born with is the ability to learn and grow. You hold the power to your happiness, you hold the power to your success and this is your life and your story! Your attention will determine your direction. Your actions will demand results. Your attitude will determine your future. It is up to you to knock on the door or how else can it be opened. You can start by praying and listening to inspirational music and messages, then try reading and setting aside some devotional time to meditate. As you open the door to spiritual growth personalizes your spiritual growth to fit your life. Sing and worship as much as you need to, pray and meditate as much as you need to, read and study as much as you need to. If any other human being is capable of growing spiritually, experiencing grace and mercy, peace and love why are you any different?

"Grace and peace be multiplied unto you through the knowledge of God, and Jesus our Lord. According to as his divine power hath given unto us all things that pertain unto life and godliness, through the knowledge of him that hath called us to glory and virtue: Whereby are given unto us exceeding great and precious promises: that by these ye might be partakers of the divine nature, having escaped the corruption that is in the world through lust. And beside this, giving all diligence, add to your faith virtue; and to virtue knowledge; And to knowledge temperance; and to temperance patience; and to patience godliness; And to godliness brotherly kindness; and to brotherly kindness charity. For if these things are in you, and abound, they make you that ye shall neither be barren nor unfruitful in the knowledge of our Lord

Prayer:

God I thank you for a spirit of power love and a sound mind. Please create in me a clean heart and renew a right spirit in me.

Jesus Christ." 2 Peter 1: 2-8

Maybe you're thinking "God could never love me I've sinned too much". Or maybe you think "What God, I've never seen him, he doesn't exist". Maybe you are afraid of what people around you will think if they see you smiling, free from stress, and acting differently walking in the faith. Guess what! None of these can stop your spiritual growth. The only thing that can stop you from spiritual growth and salvation is you. Your sins are forgiven in Christ. No sin of the past is a reason or disqualification to oppose peace, spiritual growth, and being a better you. One thing you will learn in your journey of spiritual growth is grace. While the goal of religion is to walk the straight and narrow and to let go of bad habits nobody is perfect. Some of us have allowed guilt, pain, fear, and anger to rob us of joy and peace that is so easily accessible through Christ Jesus. Mercy is available all you need to do is ask, confess your sins, and commit yourself unto the Lord. Forgive yourself and ask for forgiveness from those whom you have hurt. Ask and receive the forgiveness that is available to you. You may not be able to see, smell, touch, or even taste the Holy Spirit but you can feel and hear the spirit. You can speak in your mind and hear in your mind without moving your tongue while also having earplugs in. That is your spiritual being. How can you hear the spirit, your spirit, and deny the existence of God's spirit? It doesn't make any sense, does it? How can the wind which you can't see, or taste exist? How can emotions which can be felt but not seen exist? You can't see the time, yet the clock keeps on ticking. It is up to you to acknowledge God and his existence because whether you choose to believe God exists or not does not change the fact that he exists. Not only does he exist, but he wants you to live your best life.

"For God so loved the world that he gave his only begotten Son, that whosoever believeth in him should not perish but have everlasting life. For God sent not his Son into the world to condemn the world; but that the world through him might be saved." John 3:16-17

"For all have sinned, and come short of the glory of God; being justified freely by his grace through the redemption that is in Christ Jesus. Whom God hath set forth to be a propitiation through faith in his blood to declare his righteousness for the remission of sins that are in the past through the forbearance of God." Romans 3:23-25

Focus

To focus we must first put things into a clear perspective. Just like someone looking through a telescope or having a vision test for corrective lenses some steps should be taken before we can focus. Some of us fall victim to an idol mind. It is important to use your mind the way God intended which is to see things in the spirit, so it can be manifested in the natural. Our minds are also for knowledge, wisdom, and understanding so we can hear with our spiritual ears and comprehend the substance and word of God. We carry inside of us, the ability to use our minds to plan initiate, and implement the principles God set before us in his word so that we can live an abundant life. God gives us understanding, and the ability to apply that knowledge and understanding to our daily living. Your attention will determine your direction. Your actions will demand results. Your attitude will determine your future. We can choose to move in faith and to move in purpose or we can choose not to, to be lazy. There is a bible verse in the book of Matthew and it teaches a very important message. The message is that he who is faithful with little is given much. When we use the tools and talents that God has selflessly given us to help others and to grow we not only help others, but we also help ourselves. The more we apply our knowledge, our talents, and our monies the more knowledge talent and money God will trust us with. It is up to us to implement this not only in our finances but also in our learning and giving. Laziness displeases God.

Like the master in the book of Matthew God wants us to enter in his Joy. His joy is far better and magnificent than any joy we can provide ourselves. First, he wants us to do well with what we have. He wants us to operate in faith and to master the responsibilities, talents, and monies he has already entrusted us with. Too often we put limits on ourselves with doubt, fear, laziness, regret, false pleasure and so many other things that can deter us from focusing on doing our best. I can remember how excited I was in class in school always focused on the lesson, full of questions, hoping to understand and obtain the correct answer. I knew that there was a reward for learning. I'd be to get an A instead of a C. I would be able to give the other students understanding as opposed to asking for help. Most importantly I would have knowledge that I could carry forward with me and apply in life.

Blindly enthusiastic about learning, I didn't realize because I was faithful with the knowledge God had given me I would be able to go on to special gifted and talented meetings and trips because I was faithful in the little he had given me. When you take what you've got invest in it, master it, and apply it, it is multiplied. When you have a genuine appreciation for what you have God wants to add to it. God wants us to put our faith into action. We are expected to put forth an effort to work what we have, to help others, and to trust that God knows how much we can bear in responsibilities, talents, and monies. God wants us to enter in his joy with meekness instead of pride, with love instead of lust, with others in mind instead of only ourselves, with trust instead of fear.

In all labor there is profit, but mere talk leads only to poverty." Proverbs 14:23

"You will keep in perfect peace those whose minds are steadfast, because they trust in you," Isaiah 26:3

"For it will be like a man going on a journey, who called his servants and entrusted to them his property. To one he gave five talents, to another two, to another one, to each according to his ability. Then he went away. He who had received the five talents went at once and traded with them, and he made five talents more. So also he who had the two talents made two talents more. But he who had received the one talent went and dug in the ground and hid his master's money. Now after a long time, the master of those servants came and settled accounts with them. And he who had received the five talents came forward, bringing five talents more, saying, 'Master, you delivered to me five talents; here, I have made five talents more.' His master said to him, 'Well done, good and faithful servant. You have been faithful over a little; I will set you over much. Enter into the joy of your master.' And he also who had the two talents came forward, saying, 'Master, you delivered to me two talents; here, I have made two talents more.' His master said to him, 'Well done, good and faithful servant. You have been faithful over a little; I will set you over much. Enter into the joy of your master.' He

also who had received the one talent came forward, saying, 'Master, I knew you to be a hard man, reaping where you did not sow, and gathering where you scattered no seed, so I was afraid, and I went and hid your talent in the ground. Here, you have what is yours.' But his master answered him, 'You wicked and slothful servant! You knew that I reap where I have not sown and gather where I scattered no seed? Then you ought to have invested my

money with the bankers, and at my coming, I should have received what was my own with interest. So take the talent from him and give it to him who has the ten talents. For everyone who has will more be given, and he will have an abundance. But from the one who has not, even what he has will be taken away. And cast the worthless servant into the outer darkness. In that place, there will be weeping and gnashing of teeth.' "Matthew 25:14-
30

"In everything I did, I showed you that by this kind of hard work we must help the weak, remembering the words the Lord Jesus himself said: 'It is more blessed to give than to receive.'" Acts 20: 35

In the same light, God wants us to find a balance between abounding and hungry to abound is to have more than enough, and to have more than enough means that you can give. So, in essence, we should be content and a cheerful giver. If we abound, while we may be able to sustain with what we currently have, the more we have the more we are able to give. To hunger is to have a strong desire or craving for. If you're hungry you will work, hunt, and cook to eat. You would put forth an effort that surpasses the norm. So, in essence, we should crave and desire to be more and have more even known we will be required of more. Jesus could have said to his Father I don't want any of your glory, I don't want to be the prince of peace, I don't want to be a healer because it just too much work. Instead, he took on the responsibility, and the knowledge and the glory that came along with the heavy-duty of being the savior. Think about the focus that took. How did he do it? He did it by seeking God and by standing on the word and God's promises. Once you put things into perspective, you will suddenly find that you have more than enough to sustain yet you also have the hunger to do what you are called to do. In Christ you are rich or and you don't need anything, yet you hunger for greatness to please the father. When you have that perspective, that's when you set a goal and go after it. At that time with that balance, you master and focus on the task at hand. There will be times, especially if you are only beginning to focus when you forget what it is that you are supposed to be doing or could be doing. That's ok but now that you are aware and know what needs to change or what needs to be done, it is up to you to act. Start planning, writing, practicing, and doing a little at a time and as you plan ask God to order your steps.

Write your own prayer. Focus on your
heart and ask God to give you wisdom
and focus.

Rejoice in the Lord always

And again I say, Rejoice. Let your moderation be known unto all men. The Lord is at hand. Be careful of nothing, but in everything by prayer and supplication with thanksgiving let your requests be made known unto God. And the peace of God, which passeth all understanding, shall keep your hearts and minds through Christ Jesus. 8 Finally, brethren, whatsoever things are true, whatsoever things are honest, whatsoever things are just, whatsoever things are pure, whatsoever things are lovely, whatsoever things are of good report; if there be any virtue, and if there be any praise, think on these things. Those things, which ye have both learned, and received, and heard, and seen in me, do: and the God of peace shall be with you. But I rejoiced in the Lord greatly, that now at the last your care of me hath flourished again; wherein ye were also careful, but ye lacked opportunity. Not that I speak in respect of want: for I have learned, in whatsoever state I am, therewith to be content. I know both how to be abased, and I know how to abound: everywhere and in all things, I am instructed both to be full and to be hungry, both to abound and to suffer need. I can do all things through Christ which strengthened me. Notwithstanding ye have well done, that ye did communicate with my affliction. Now ye Philippians know also, that at the beginning of the gospel when I departed from Macedonia, no church communicated with me as concerning giving and receiving, but ye only. For even in Thessalonica ye sent once and again unto my necessity. Not because I desire a gift: but I desire fruit that may abound to your account. But I have all and abound: I am full, having received of Epaphroditus the things which were sent from you, an odour of a sweet smell, a sacrifice acceptable, well-pleasing to God. But my God shall supply all your need according to his riches in glory by Christ Jesus. Now unto God and our Father be glory forever and ever. Amen. "Philippians 4: 4-20

Some of us just need help. Unfortunately, there›s this thing called pride and it can cause you to be in denial at times. Pride can be such an ugly trait.

Pride will sometimes disguise itself as confidence but know the difference.

Just as lust tries to disguise itself as love, know the difference. It is important to be confident but equally as important to be humble. We should place our confidence in Christ, and in knowing how he sees us. Do not be afraid to ask God for help. Be receptive when God sends you help and gives you direction.

"But seek ye first the kingdom of God and his righteousness, and all these things shall be added unto you." Matthew 6:33

"Ask, and it shall be given you; seek, and ye shall find; knock, and it shall be opened unto you: For every one that asketh receiveth; and he that seeketh. findeth; and to him that knocketh it shall be opened." Matthew: 7-8

Resources

57

For book publishing, contact B&B Publishing Co
469-632-6384

Credit Services Learn more at
www.prosperityprincesscredit.com

Financial Capital Services Learn more at
www.prosperityprincesscapital.com

Credit Business Oppertunities Join Prosperity Princess
www.prosperityprincesscreditagent.com

Scientists and Mentor Learn more at
http://prettygirlworld.org

Spiritual Pastor Paul Morrisey
Freedom Church
www.freedomchurchcapecode.com

Spiritual
Freedom Church
www.freedomchurchcapecode.com